*Leadership Lessons:*
# THINGS I WISH THEY'D TOLD ME

*Leadership Lessons: Things I Wish They'd Told Me*

Copyright © 2017 Dr. Ron Webb. All rights reserved.

No rights claimed for public domain material, all rights reserved. No parts of this publication may be reproduced, stored in any retrieval system, or transmitted in any form or by any means, electronic, mechanical, recording, or otherwise, without the prior written permission of the author. Violations may be subject to civil or criminal penalties.

Unless stated otherwise, all Scriptures are taken from the King James Version of the Holy Bible © 1984 by Thomas Nelson, Inc. Used by permission.

Library of Congress Control Number: 2017945522

ISBN:   978-1-63308-272-4 Paperback
        978-1-63308-273-1 Digital

*Interior and Cover Design by* R'tor John D. Maghuyop

1028 S Bishop Avenue, Dept. 178
Rolla, MO 65401

Printed in United States of America

Author of *Leadership From Behind the Scenes*
# DR. RON WEBB

## *Leadership Lessons:*
# THINGS I WISH THEY'D TOLD ME

CHALFANT ECKERT

PUBLISHING

# TABLE OF CONTENTS

INTRODUCTION ..................................................... 7

CHAPTER 1:  I Wish They'd Told Me Seminary Alone Won't Prepare You for Ministry .............................................. 11

CHAPTER 2:  I Wish They'd Told Me It's Okay to Have a Sense of Humor (In fact, it's necessary) ....................... 19

CHAPTER 3:  I Wish They'd Told Me That There Will Be Disappointments ................. 25

CHAPTER 4:  I Wish They'd Told Me There Will Be Seasons in the Ministry ....... 33

CHAPTER 5:  I Wish They'd Told Me There Will Be Attacks and Betrayal ........... 41

CHAPTER 6:  I Wish They'd Told Me Folks Aren't That Quick to Forgive Preachers ...... 47

CHAPTER 7:  I Wish They'd Told Me That People in Leadership Will Be Offended ...... 53

CHAPTER 8:  I Wish They'd Told Me That People Can Be Vicious ..................... 59

CHAPTER 9:    I Wish They'd Told Me That
                There Will Be Drama......................65

CHAPTER 10:  I Wish They'd Told Me The
                Challenges and Burdens of
                Building and Business ....................71

CHAPTER 11:  I Wish They'd Told Me
                The Importance of Rest...................79

EPILOGUE:    I Wish They Told Me
                And the List Goes On . . ..................91

REFERENCES........................................................95

ABOUT THE AUTHOR.........................................97

# INTRODUCTION

When seasoned men and women share their experiences, their helpfulness toward others is boundless. The information you will gather from these pages will literally change your life. From these pages, I am certain you will find tidbits that will greatly encourage you as a leader, pastor, youth pastor, or CEO of a business or corporation.

It's amazing to me the many ways we are all so much alike. I often wonder why we magnify our differences instead of embracing our similarities and cultivating them. In my many conversations with pastors, bishops, elders, business leaders—along with those who have served and held positions of authority in the armed services—I have found that we share many of the same experiences.

That awareness inspired me to interview nearly 100 pastors and businessmen and women, as well as other people holding leadership positions. During these one-on-one conversations, both face-to-face and by phone, I could feel the hurt, rejection, loneliness, isolation, betrayal, and discouragement these leaders faced. And while the pain they experienced was primarily due to being the "top dog," one thing became abundantly clear—pain is pain regardless of the position someone might hold.

In my ministry, I'm on the road a lot, and I get to meet people from all walks of life as I preach the Gospel and conduct leadership conferences. I recently took a busy and exciting tour that included an appearance on Trinity Broadcasting Network, along with stops in Tennessee, Texas, Missouri, Arkansas, Kentucky, Virginia, North

Carolina, Delaware, and Pennsylvania makes me want to sing the old Hank Snow song, *I've Been Everywhere* (Mack, 1959). During this trip, I was struck by a clear revelation. Although I was on assignment preaching, teaching, and book signing, I noticed that many of the pastors I met had the same burning questions concerning the challenges they were having as leaders.

Many of these ministers of the Gospel were young pastors, and they were clearly craving a real mentor. Many of them felt like they were too inexperienced and ill-equipped to deal with the multitude of challenges that come with leading a ministry. I recall one pastor who experienced feelings of failure and shared that he wanted to resign every Monday. Others confessed how they had prepared their letters of resignation but hadn't submitted them yet. I came across those who admitted they were simply worn out, having grown tired in well doing. And I even had some confess that they had entertained suicide.

These glimpses into the realities of ministry burdened my heart and became so great that I felt led by God to prepare a manual for new leaders about to enter the ministry, and for those already in leadership. I believe this manual can be an essential tool that will prepare you for the myriad of leadership challenges you will face in ministry and business. I truly believe it can be a tool to rescue the lives and ministries of God's chosen leaders.

Over 75 percent of the pastors I interviewed, regardless of their age or years of experience, expressed the same frustration: "I wish I had known this information before I started." If you find yourself feeling like they do or if you've come to the realization that leadership requires both a lifeline and an anchor (when you throw out a lifeline to others, you need to be anchored yourself in order to remain stable enough to hold yourself together), you will find plenty of helpful insight in the pages of this manual.

Welcome to the ministry.

*Dr. Ron Webb*

# CHAPTER 1

# I Wish They'd Told Me

## *Seminary Alone Won't Prepare You for Ministry*

Only a church guided by the Holy Spirit can truly qualify a man or woman to serve in the ministry. Leading God's people is unlike any other task in the world, which is why it requires the calling of the Holy Spirit in addition to education and training for the job.

As guardians of life, medical doctors have a very stressful job, and their decisions can mean life or death in some cases. As guardians of eternal life, a pastor has the awesome responsibility of dealing with the immortal soul of man, and their decisions have the potential to affect eternity. The pastor carries the greater burden.

Medical school prepares a doctor "on paper" to treat the body, but that doesn't mean he will be successful when it comes to the actual treatment of a patient. In the same manner, seminary prepares a pastor to lead the body of Christ "on paper," but it doesn't mean he will be successful when it comes to actually leading the people.

## Undefined Role

Funny how people think they know our job description. Even though new pastors often find themselves wearing several different hats, most congregations haven't defined the role they expect their pastor to play; and many times, they don't even know what the pastor's role is. I have personally experienced this, as have many of the pastors I interviewed. I've served on a church board charged with finding a new pastor, and there have been situations where the expectations of the congregation and the expectations of the person applying for the position have been miles apart from each other.

While some churches expect a great preacher like the Apostle Paul—able to effectively articulate and communicate the Word—too many churches are looking for pastors who will meet each and every possible need. If they're sad, preach something to make them happy. If they're sick, preach something to heal them. If they're down, preach something to pick them up. If they are in trouble, preach something motivational to give them peace.

If we aren't careful, we could end up allowing the followers to tell the leader what he should preach, even though we should always rely on the Holy Spirit to lead us as we prepare our message.

You can almost hear the congregation saying, "Never mind your personal issues, your family issues, your financial issues, or your marital issues. Just preach, Sir! That's what you're supposed to do; preach and preach some more."

On the other hand, there are those who feel like we should be motivational speakers who will tickle their ears and make them feel happy—although there's nothing wrong about preaching happy, motivational sermons when the Spirit leads.

*And the LORD answered me, and said,
Write the vision, and make it plain upon tables,
that he may run that readeth it. For the vision is
yet for an appointed time, but at the end it shall
speak, and not lie: though it tarry, wait for it;
because it will surely come, it will not tarry.*
—Habakkuk 2: 3-4

Proverbs 29:18 tells us that, "Where there is no vision, the people perish." Of course, God speaks to us as leaders, and when He does, we speak to the people, but the leader needs to be allowed to lead. Sometimes congregations demand what Scripture clearly doesn't support.

Some people expect their pastor to equip and lead them. I feel these are the most important and Scriptural needs of today's church (Ephesians 4:12-13), and they are the two most neglected. It is the pastor's job to equip the saints for the work of the ministry—not to marry everyone in the church or preach at every funeral. We are responsible for preparing the people to do these things.

Many congregations expect the pastor's family to be fully involved in his work. I don't know of any other private sector job that requires such extensive family involvement. For example, the school board doesn't demand that the high school principal's wife help decorate the hallways or attend basketball games, but many churches have such expectations for the pastor's wife and children. Keep in mind that I do believe they should be involved in some activities. But when the pastor's family fails to meet these unreasonable expectations, many churches become disenchanted with them, as well as the pastor, whether their disappointments are real or imagined.

Many congregations have the unreasonable expectation that the pastor's children should be perfect, but they need encouragement just like every child does. When we look in the Bible, we find that many of the leaders called of God had children that rebelled.

1. Eli's sons didn't support him (I Samuel 2:12-26).
2. Samuel's son didn't support him (I Samuel 8:1-3).
3. David's sons rebelled against him (II Samuel 13).

## Difficulties of Leadership and Friendship

One of the greatest challenges facing church leaders today is finding and maintaining close relationships and friendships. It doesn't take long before pastors discover how hard it is to walk the tightrope of leadership and friendship. Leaders and their families often find it difficult to find friends they can confide in, and they often feel betrayed by those closest to them—giving rise to jealousy and resentment while destroying the relationship. Sadly, this can happen even when the friendship is with another minister.

## NOW THAT I KNOW

1. Think of a person with excellent leadership skills.

   _____

   a. How do you feel when you are around that person?

   _____

   _____

   _____

   b. What leadership traits do you most admire about him or her?

   _____

   _____

   _____

   c. What can you learn from this person?

   _____

   _____

   _____

   _____

d. How can you emulate the traits you appreciate most?

2. How do you help young leaders develop leadership skills? How do you build friendships and mentoring relationships to bless these young leaders?

3. Think of a situation you have been involved in for which leadership was sorely lacking?

a. How did you handle it?

_____

_____


b. What could have done differently to get a different outcome?

_____

_____

_____


c. Why do you think leadership was lacking in that situation?

_____

_____

_____


4. Think about the typical atmospheres at home and at church. If you were to interject better leadership on a regular basis, how would those atmospheres change?

_____

_____

_____

5. How can you use your leadership skills to inspire and benefit those around you?

   _____

   _____

   _____

   _____

# CHAPTER 2

# I WISH THEY'D TOLD ME

## *It's Okay to Have a Sense of Humor (In fact, it's necessary)*

Laughter is a gift from God; it can even improve your health. Proverbs 17:22 (KJV) says, "A merry heart doeth good like a medicine: but a broken spirit drieth the bones." In this line of work that we call *ministry*, there can be lots of pain, lots of hurts, and lots of stress. Sometimes, the burden of dealing with this reality causes burnout (mental health) as well as sickness or disease (physical health). If our mental and physical health are suffering, it almost always influences our relationship with God (spiritual health). Therefore, it's important to do all we can to create an atmosphere of joy and relaxation as a form of stress release. To be blunt, we need to give ourselves the grace necessary to "chill out" and not take everything so seriously.

Many of the leaders I know have shared with me how learning to develop a sense of humor actually helped the people around them to loosen up. Personally, I have seen my sense of humor open many doors for me. In addition, as a leader in the fight against racial division in our land, I have personally experienced the destruction of racial barriers by simply knowing how to laugh. While many people choose to focus on the worst parts of a difficult situation, I have made it a priority to find the humor in every situation. Trust me: it's there if you look for it.

Martin Luther once said, "If God has no sense of humor, I don't want to go to heaven." Fortunately, Psalms 2:4 tells us that the One enthroned in heaven (our loving Heavenly Father) laughs. This means that when we laugh, we are showing the very character and quality of God's nature because we are created in His image. Laughter is a gift; it's a natural component of our nature, and it should play an active role in living a life of fulfillment and happiness.

Humor is perhaps one of our greatest assets as leaders, and it will go a long way in helping us maintain a proper prospective in life. Men and women in leadership should be upbeat, cheerful, pleasant, optimistic, open, and positive—essential characteristics to possess and maintain a healthy sense of humor. I'm not talking about being a stand-up comic, although there's nothing wrong with that. Simply learning to loosen up can often transform a tense situation into a positive one as we create an atmosphere of understanding and laughter.

I remember a situation from nearly 30 years ago. I was given the privilege of speaking to a group in a small town where absolutely no African Americans lived. I could feel the stares when I approached the stage, and while it would have been easy for me to feel intimidated, I used my sense of humor to break the ice and relieve the tension by saying, "There's a lot of white lightning in here, but a chocolate thunder has just arrived." People laughed so hard they cried, and as a result, the whole room loosened up.

It was as if God was telling me, "Don't take everything so seriously. Chill out, relax, and take one day at a time."

Some of the most emotional and difficult times for those in the ministry come when we must preach at a funeral because the loss of a loved one is a hard thing to deal with. Yet, I remember on more than one occasion how, right in the middle of the sadness and tears, simply sharing a funny story would cause an outburst of laughter. Those in attendance would often come up to me after the service to shake my hand, saying, "Thank you so much. I really needed that."

Too often in life we put on a fake persona to hide who we really are. We think that if we can impress others by looking or acting the part, we will find acceptance in their eyes. It rarely works.

So, let me challenge you right now to start living out the dream and vision given to you by the One who knows you, loves you, and calls you to leadership. And when you do, be sure you remember to laugh your way to heaven.

Here are some more benefits of laughter:

1. A sense of humor will improve your social circle. You will live a healthier and happier life.
2. It will attract people to you. People like to laugh as a technique to get rid of stress and just have a good time, and they enjoy hanging around people who make them laugh.
3. Laughter is the perfect cure for dealing with stress. Stress is a part of all our lives, and the more we have to do, the more stress we have. Laughter causes our bodies to produce endorphins (the body's natural pain reliever). It relaxes blood vessels and increases blood flow which is the perfect antidote to tension.

Even though there are other stress-relieving activities, nothing gets rid of stress like a good belly laugh.
4. Laughter improves the immune system (which helps to fight infection), relaxes the muscles, lowers blood pressure, and reduces the chance of a heart attack.
5. According to a study by the University of London of Neurology, laughter can activate the part of the brain that is important for learning and comprehending (Mcgettigan, et al., 2013).
6. Laughter diffuses anger and can be a bond of friendship to enjoy for all eternity. In my conclusion: Remember to not take life too seriously and learn to laugh. Just laugh! As Job 8:21 reminds us, "He will once again fill your mouth with laughter and your lips with shouts of joy" (New Living Translation).

## NOW THAT I KNOW

1. Think of a person with a good sense of humor. How do you feel when you are around that person?

   _____

   _____

   _____

2. Recall a situation that was especially tense.

   a. How did you handle it?

   _____

   _____

   _____

   b. What could you have done differently to get a different outcome?

   _____

   _____

   _____

c. How could you have used humor to diffuse the tension?

_____

_____

_____

3. Think about the typical atmospheres at home and at church. If you were to interject humor on a regular basis, how would those atmospheres change?

_____

_____

_____

4. How can you use humor to inspire those around you?

_____

_____

_____

# CHAPTER 3

# I Wish They'd Told Me

## *That There Will Be Disappointments*

Disappointment is a reality of life, and many of us learn how to handle it. But if we're not careful, it can catch us by surprise. Some paint a picture of the ministry that makes it look inviting, and that's okay because there are many great things to be experienced as leaders. But we also need to think of our calling like the local military recruiting officer—the job can sound good and inviting, but we better not forget the basic training that comes along with it.

A lot of us know how it feels to have our dreams shattered and our plans interrupted. Sometimes, if we're not careful, disappointment can be so crushing that it leaves us emotionally scarred for life.

On the other hand, many people show us how to rise above the disappointment of a broken vision or shattered dream and live in victory. Let me introduce to you a man who faced life-long disappointments and yet triumphed over it all.

If there was ever a man who experienced disappointments and personal tragedy, it was the Prophet Jeremiah. Already called to serve at a difficult time in the history of God's people (he witnessed the fall of Jerusalem and the destruction of

Solomon's temple), Jeremiah was given a very unpopular and difficult message to proclaim—to warn God's people and the nation that judgment was coming and that they needed to repent or be cast out of Judah.

Despite facing discouragement and depression, along with the incredible anguish of being rejected by those he was called to warn, Jeremiah served the Lord faithfully for many years. Through it all, he never compromised in his message or his loyalty to God and His people.

Because of the unpopular and convicting message God called him to give, Jeremiah's friends turned against him; and my friend, your friends will turn against you too. That can be tremendously disappointing. It's important to remember that not everyone who starts with you will stay with you. Just as Peter broke his promise to Jesus when he said he would die before ever denying him (Matthew 26:35), you'll come across those who promise to stay with you through thick and thin only to abandon you when you need them the most. Family will forsake you, but not only family; friends will turn on you too. That is what happened to Jeremiah as he experienced one hurt after another; and in the end, the entire nation turned against him. Though he followed his calling to the very end, Jeremiah saw his nation overrun by the enemy.

Jeremiah's calling led to his broken heart, and the book bearing his name gives witness of the burdens he carried. He also wrote the book of Lamentations that has his tear stains on almost every verse (he was known as "The Weeping Prophet"). Jeremiah saw everything fall apart, and he could have died a bitter or broken man. Instead, his life served as one of the greatest declarations of faith and faithfulness found anywhere in the Bible.

Life isn't always going to be sunny and clear. There will be stormy and dark days. There will be lonely days and nights filled with challenges. None of us will escape disappointments in life; we all will face them at one time or another. Still, we can make it to the end if we remember that there will be disappointments that can be dealt with.

The Bible shows us that many of God's people faced disappointments but persevered.

1. Abraham was disappointed in the behavior of Lot, his nephew. Even though Lot had prospered under his uncle, he chose to separate from Abraham and pitch his tent toward Sodom (Genesis 13:12). We all know what happened to Sodom and Gomorrah. Even so, God promised to bless Abraham's descendants forever (Genesis 13:14-17).
2. Joseph was disappointed at the selfish treatment of his brothers who sold him out (Genesis 37). Yet, even after experiencing several trials, Joseph rose to become the second most powerful man in Egypt next to Pharaoh (Genesis 41).
3. Though called by God to deliver the Israelites from their slavery in Egypt, Moses' heart was repeatedly broken by their sin of unbelief. At one point, his frustration was so great that he wanted to die (Numbers 11).
4. King David had great plans for his family, yet some of his sons were so sinful they almost wrecked the nation (II Samuel, Chapters 16-19).
5. Job was the richest man in Land of Uz, was on top of the world, and everything was going great. But in less than twenty-four hours, his whole world turned upside down.

He lost everything: his fortune, his family, his livestock. He lost oxen and sheep, which represented his fortune (Job 1). He also lost his influence, but he didn't lose his praise. Job said, "The Lord giveth and the Lord taketh away. Blessed be the name of the Lord." Now that's an attitude of a winner. If you fall eight times, get up nine.

Just like these great men of the Bible, we will face disappointments that will try to rattle our faith. Still, if we take up the "full armor of God," we can stand firm (Ephesians 6:13) and know with confidence that we can overcome any disappointment that comes our way.

Before a football coach creates his game plan for an upcoming game, he will study the opposition to know what he's likely to face when they meet. Just like that coach, it's a good thing for leaders in the ministry to study as well. That way, they can enter the game knowing what to expect.

Jesus said it this way:

> *For which of you, intending to build a tower, sitteth not down first, and counteth the cost, whether he have sufficient to finish it? Lest haply, after he hath laid the foundation, and is not able to finish it, all that behold it begin to mock him, saying, "This man began to build, and was not able to finish." Or what king, going to make war against another king, sitteth not down first, and consulteth whether he be able with ten thousand to meet him that cometh against him with twenty thousand? Or else, while the other is yet a great way off, he sendeth an ambassage, and desireth conditions of peace.*
> —Luke 14:28-32

It's been said that we should "plan our work and then work our plan." Disappointments will show up in many places from many sources. And while we won't necessarily know exactly when or where they will happen, if we approach the ministry with the understanding that disappointments will come, we can stand against them in victory.

Don't lose faith or throw in the towel. Pray through it, fight through it, and work through it.

## NOW THAT I KNOW

1. Think of a deep disappointment you have endured.

   _____

   _____

   _____

   _____

   a. What were the reasons for this disappointment?

   _____

   _____

   _____

   _____

   b. How did you handle it?

   _____

   _____

   _____

   _____

c. What could you have done differently to get a different outcome?

_____

_____

_____

_____

d. What did you learn from the disappointment?

_____

_____

_____

_____

2. How often do you find yourself disappointed? Is it occasional or has it become a way of life?

_____

_____

_____

_____

3. How can you use your disappointments to positively influence and motivate those around you?

   _____

   _____

   _____

   _____

4. Sum up your philosophy about disappointment in one sentence.

   _____

   _____

   _____

   _____

5. Is your philosophy God-centered or self-centered? Explain.

   _____

   _____

   _____

   _____

# CHAPTER 4

# I Wish They'd Told Me

## *There Will Be Seasons in the Ministry*

In Ecclesiastes 3:1, we learn that to everything there is a season. And in Genesis 8:22, we learn that, "While the earth remaineth, seed time and harvest, and cold and heat, and summer and winter, and day and night shall not cease." (KJV)

Leaders in the ministry need to know that the work they do will go through seasons, and that these seasons will exist as long as the earth remains. God established them, and regardless of what we think or how we feel about them, we must respect each season and know that as they come, they have a purpose designed to help us mature. We can't pray away or prophesy away seasons we don't like. But if we allow, seasons can help us to know where we are and where we're going. We don't want to get stuck in a particular season, nor do we want to overstay our time there.

So, how do we know when a change in seasons is coming? We need to ask God and follow His lead, because He alone changes the time and season (Daniel 2). When we do that, we can rest in the knowledge that, through it all, God is in control of everything.

Sometimes we might be fortunate enough to do the "right" thing in the "wrong" season. In other words, it's possible for us to birth something out of season. For example, we might embark on a new beginning (Spring season) when we should be waiting on the Lord (Winter season). But our greatest successes will come when we operate in the season God has us in.

It's always in our best interest to know what season we're in so we can do the right thing at the right time. When we do, we can be as the sons of Issachar, men who understood the times and seasons, and knew what Israel was supposed to do (I Chronicles 12:32).

In every season, we need to humbly seek God for His guidance because every season can conceal a matter or reveal a matter. When we take the time to understand the season we are in, we'll know if it's time to move forward or time to stand still; we'll know how long we need to hold on and when it's time to let go. We must surrender control and cease from trying to manipulate the seasons. We don't know, nor can we control, how long a season will last. But because we know God is in control of our lives, we can know what to do and when to do it.

When we insist on taking control of the driver's seat, any season can quickly become a season of frustration; the spirit of confusion can then take over, and we can end up questioning God.

On the other hand, it's important to remember that Satan is fully aware that God has called us to lead His people, and He's always looking for someone to devour (I Peter 5:8). One of Satan's favorite tools is confusion, so it's also helpful if we remember that confusion doesn't come from God (I Corinthians 14:33). If confusion is having its way, we need to keep on keepin' on, even when it seems like everything we do is wrong.

Some of our frustration is caused by our own selfish choices. The Apostle Paul had seasons in his life (Romans 7:14-17) when he was frustrated and confused due to his struggle between doing good (God's will) and doing evil (his fleshly will). But Paul knew that in Christ he could still be victorious (Romans 8:1).

Jonah ended up in the belly of a great fish because of his own disobedience, his own poor choice. (Jonah 1). Yet, Jonah eventually came to his senses (Jonah 2) and followed God's calling (Jonah 3). Like Jonah, we need to take responsibility for our decisions, whether good or bad, and just own it.

It's easy to get frustrated when we step out of God's will; we turn left when God says to turn right. It's easy to lose focus and become side tracked by the enemy when we suffer from our self-inflicted wounds.

"I caused this pain in my life"

"I created this chaos in my home."

"I lost the job because I was late to work."

"I walked away from my ministry prematurely."

Even when we find ourselves in these situations, we need to ask God to forgive it and not re-live it; to rise up instead of giving up; and to move up instead of moving out.

Let me remind you, my friend, that frustration can cause you to miss your season. You can miss a dental appointment; you can miss a doctor's appointment; you can miss a hair appointment; and you can even miss a bus or a plane. But don't let frustration cause you to miss your season.

We need to also remember not to compare our seasons with the seasons of others. You'll have times when it seems like everybody around you is filled with vision and flowing with leadership. Then suddenly the winds change, all hell breaks loose, and you're left alone as you wonder what in the world just happened. Don't worry. It's just a season change. You need to seek God, ask Him to guide you through your season, and let Him guide those around you in theirs.

## We Will be Tempted

Let's be clear about this sensitive subject. Jesus was tempted in every way, yet He was without sin (Hebrews 4:15). So, let's get real; if Jesus was tempted, you know we'll be tempted too. In today's society, many things spark temptation. Almost anything we could ever want is literally right at our fingertips. Push one button on your computer and there it is: sex, money, and power all wrapped up in a pretty package to feed our flesh.

By the way, temptation is not a sin; it's the yielding to it that becomes sin. But even in our moments of temptation, God provides a way to defeat it (I Corinthians 10:13). The way to fend it off is to avoid putting ourselves in hot spots. If we crave sweets, we need to stay out of the candy store. If sex is our weakness, we need to monitor our exposure to seductive stimuli of all kinds including movies and television shows. If alcohol tempts us, we need to avoid driving by the liquor store.

Remember, the devil knows what to send our way. He knows what we like and how we like it! It's for this reason that Jesus tells us to take up our cross every day (Luke 9:23). When we crucify our flesh every day, can we be victorious over temptation (Galatians 5:24). We can also be victorious over the desires of the flesh when we choose to walk in the Spirit (Galatians 5:16).

## Sexual Temptation

Sexual temptation can be very strong, and it's made worse by television. It's nearly impossible to watch a movie or a sporting event without seeing someone half naked, even in the commercials. Marketing experts have learned that anyone can sell any product if it's attached to sex. As leaders, we can't allow ourselves to succumb to that temptation.

I'm often reminded that the strongest man in the Bible was taken down by sexual temptation. Samson once slew a thousand Philistines with nothing but the jaw bone of a donkey (Judges 15:15), yet he wasn't strong enough to resist one woman. Even though Samson was a judge of Israel for twenty years (Judges 15:20), in the end he was destroyed because he chose not to avoid temptation (Judges 16).

King David, a man after God's own heart (Act 13:22), was mightily anointed by God. Scripture tells us about how David killed lions and bears (I Samuel 17:36), killed Goliath (I Samuel 17:45-49) and many other giants (II Samuel 21:15-22). But David couldn't fight his lusts (II Samuel 11-24).

## There's a reason for your season

There's a reason for your season, whether it's good, bad, or ugly.

- A test today will become a testimony tomorrow.
- Today's pain will become tomorrow's power.
- Your struggle will become your strength and your sorrow will turn to joy.

Even if you mess up, God will use your seasons to work everything together for your good and according to His purpose for your life (Romans 8:28). There's a reason you went through what you went through; there's a reason you suffered what you suffered.

There's a reason because there's a season.

## Season of Waiting

No one enjoys waiting; it makes us impatient and irritable. But just as the farmer must wait for the seed to grow before he can harvest his crops, we need to realize that waiting is a key to building our ministry. If you get nothing else from this chapter, remember that waiting is not a waste; it's simply a part of the process. God has set an appointed time to bring your promise to pass, so don't become weary in well doing (Galatians 6:9).

No one explained to me when I started pastoring that waiting was part of the preparation, but now I'm so glad I didn't get what I wanted . . . when I wanted it. There have been lots of things I prayed for but didn't receive right away. The truth is that I wasn't ready for them. During those seasons, I learned how to keep my down time from becoming frown time. And in those times of waiting, God prepared me for what He had in store.

Know that your waiting is never in vain. Even though the fulfillment of your vision may tarry, wait on it because it will surely come to pass. God's promises may appear to be delayed, but they are never denied. Wait it out and walk it out. And when your breakthrough comes, it will be well worth it.

## NOW THAT I KNOW

1. List the seasons of your life from birth to now:

   a. _____

   b. _____

   c. _____

   d. _____

   e. _____

   f. _____

2. When you look back from one season to another, can you identify specific events or things that happened that caused the transition? Were your actions (good or bad) responsible for the timing of the season change?

   _____

   _____

   _____

   _____

   _____

3. During seasons of sorrow, lack, or hurt, what did you learn about your Christian walk that helped move you to a happier season?

_____

_____

_____

4. How can your experiences with changing seasons inspire those around you to hang in and wait for the transition?

_____

_____

_____

# CHAPTER 5

# I WISH THEY'D TOLD ME

## *There Will Be Attacks and Betrayal*

Have you ever had someone say something unkind to you or about you? I think we've all experienced it at one time or another. Being the victim of slander or malicious gossip can be difficult to bear. However, the good news is that God conditions us to handle such situations.

I can't begin to tell you how many of my friends and family members have been victims of these deadly attacks. I use the word *deadly* because life and death are in the power of the tongue (Proverbs 18:21). I feel a great deal of empathy for people who have been assaulted by negative or cruel words because I have had similar experiences. When word got back to me about what was said against me, my feelings alternated between despondency and anger, even though I knew I needed to count it as all joy (Matthew 5:10-12).

In my opinion, one of the greatest books ever written about the virtue of love in the Christian life is Jonathan Edwards' book, *Charity and Its Fruits* (Edwards, 2013). Edwards includes a chapter on how we are to respond to false charges, how such attacks shouldn't surprise us, and how we should actually expect them. He also points out that if the

Christian expects slander and keeps his eyes on God, when it happens, he will not be depressed over it.

Edwards accurately points out that only worldly pleasures (i.e. health, money, reputation) can be harmed by the slander of others. These things all have to do with the pleasures and cares of this world, but we have an inheritance laid up in Heaven—a treasure no one can steal or destroy (Matthew 6:19-21), and it's protected by the Lord himself (I Peter 1:4).

It would be easy to think that Edwards was a spiritual giant who handled personal attacks with ease, while we are just ordinary believers struggling with bitterness and unforgiveness. We all experience distress when we are hurt by people we thought were our friends. While it's true that our human nature responds to personal attacks with sadness, anger, and bitterness, we need to respond with our spiritual nature. As leaders, we are called to walk in the fruit of the Spirit—love, joy peace, patience, kindness, goodness, faithfulness, gentleness, and self-control (Galatians 5:22-23).

We need to respond as Christ would respond because we are molded into His image (II Corinthians 3:18). Though Jesus was slandered and falsely accused of all kind of offenses, He didn't open his mouth (Isaiah 53:7). Jesus expected the attacks, and even in the movement of his passion on the cross, He prayed for the forgiveness of those who were attacking him (Luke 23:34).

That is how we're called to react to enemies; every lie ever told against us, every slander, every false accusation, and every ill word spoken against us is an opportunity to grow as we become more like Christ.

Jonathan Edwards' book helped me to see that I had allowed my soul to become distressed—which is a sin—instead of realizing that the attacks on me were an occasion to imitate Christ and grow in grace and my own edification that I might remember where my treasure is. We need to keep Edwards' insight in sight as we deal with the inevitable attacks and insults that come our way in life.

When we are attacked or betrayed, we will be left feeling hurt, abandoned, and abused if we fail to remember how we are called to respond. The gates of hell will continue to release and unleash a coordinated assault against spiritual leaders, and Satan knows that if you strike the shepherd, the sheep will scatter (Mark 14:27). For this reason, we should pray a covering around them.

Most leaders live with incredible pressure as they walk a path tougher than the path walked by those that follow. I wish someone would have warned me of the onslaught that can come against leaders in the ministry. To every leader reading these words, I hope this helps you avoid some of the heartaches waiting down the road.

## NOW THAT I KNOW

1. Recall a time when you were betrayed by someone you trusted.

   _____

   _____

   _____

   _____

   a. How did you handle it?

   _____

   _____

   _____

   b. What could you have done differently to get a different outcome?

   _____

   _____

   _____

   _____

c. How did the betrayal affect your trust in other people?

_____

_____

_____

d. What did you learn about yourself and human nature from this experience?

_____

_____

_____

e. How long did it take for you to heal from the betrayal?

_____

_____

_____

2. What does the Bible say about betrayal and trust?

_____

_____

_____

3. What Scriptures can help someone heal from being betrayed?

4. How can your experiences with treachery inspire others to persevere through their trials when people are disloyal and let them down?

# CHAPTER 6

# I Wish They'd Told Me

## *Folks Aren't That Quick to Forgive Preachers*

Forgiveness is a sensitive and often painful topic, yet dealing with it requires possessing the courage to talk about it without the emotional baggage that often comes along for the ride. In a recent meeting with a small circle of my fellow ministers, the question was asked, "How can grace work for the people in the pew but not for the pastor in the pulpit?"

My simple reply was that it can't. Grace isn't delegated or assigned based on where you sit in the church. It must be available for all, or it's available for none.

This subject hit home with many of my co-workers in the faith. They feel that life is a bit unfair because many people see the ministry as the only profession where you're not allowed to falter. We preach and teach restoration, but many in our congregations—too many—can't wait to tell us, "Don't you dare fall or make a mistake." Even though many people claim to be forgiving as they forget the wrongs of others, when it's a pastor who stumbles, too often it quickly turns into forgetting to forgive.

I recently interviewed over twenty leaders who were angry and frustrated as they labored to correct the misconception that the grace and forgiveness found in the Bible applied to the membership but not the leadership. And I must say that their feelings are common. As we take a firm stand against this misconception, it's important to remember a couple basic truths:

- Though not perfect, we are being conformed to the image of Christ, and
- Though not flawless, we are forgiven by the Blood of Christ.

We weren't perfect when we went into office. We won't be perfect while serving in office. And I doubt very seriously we will be perfect coming out of office. Yet, we can have complete assurance that we are being perfected in Christ. (Hebrews 10:14)

Even though we know we are to guard our tongues, James 3 reminds us of how important it is to tame this small member of the body. Knowing this, it can be pretty stressful for those of us in leadership to monitor every word that comes out of our mouths. It can be even more difficult when those in the flock keep a running checklist of everything we say and do as they judge our every word and deed. Often, this checklist of "wrongs" becomes the foundation for creating opinions on how they feel we should do our jobs, even though they have little knowledge of what we do or who we are.

As a result, we see many bitter, offended, and wounded leaders. The people they have extended grace to don't return the courtesy. Instead of showing grace and forgiveness, they bury their leaders with judgment and unforgiveness. They find it easier to forgive CEOs, doctors, lawyers, businessmen and businesswomen, and countless other professionals than they do to forgive those in the ministry.

Several pastors have shared with me how they followed biblical protocol by speaking with someone privately only to discover their private situation went public. Too many in the church believe that leaders aren't allowed to hurt or fully express their feelings thus leaving them abandoned, ashamed, alone, and misunderstood.

## NOW THAT I KNOW

1. Think of a time when you made a mistake and the folks in church failed to forgive you.

   _____

   _____

   _____

   a. How did you handle it?

   _____

   _____

   _____

   b. How could you have handled it differently?

   _____

   _____

   _____

   c. How long did it take for you to forgive them?

   _____

   _____

2. What does the Bible tell us about forgiveness?

   _____

   _____

   _____

3. What Scriptures can help you come to terms with unforgiveness from others and in yourself?

   _____

   _____

   _____

4. How can you use forgiveness to inspire those around you to also forgive?

   _____

   _____

   _____

# CHAPTER 7

# I Wish They'd Told Me

## *That People in Leadership Will Be Offended*

*And then shall many be offended, and shall betray one another, and shall hate one another. And many false prophets shall rise, and shall deceive many. And because iniquity shall abound, the love of many shall wax cold.*
—Matthew 24:10-12

Jesus warned us that there would be many who will be offended within the church, outside of the church, and even in our families. Did you notice that the Scripture says there will be *many*? That simply means a lot of people. Let me warn you in case you didn't know: You won't have to do anything to people to cause them to dislike you or hate you, even if you do the best you can in all situations. Sometimes, even your best won't be good enough for some people.

You'll never get away from fault finders and undermining people who will discredit you, your vision, your mission, your ministry, your marriage, your work, and even your witness. But let me encourage you not to be distracted by the actions of others. I have been in ministry for almost thirty-five years now, and never in the history of my ministry have

I experienced as many people walking in the spirit of offense as I am witnessing today.

Many people today walk around wearing their feelings on their sleeves, holding onto grudges for years, refusing to forgive those who offended them, and thinking that it's okay to behave like that. The sad thing is that many times we don't even know these people are mad or upset with us. I've watched people quit their jobs, leave their churches, stop speaking to their friends, and ruin their relationships—all because the spirit of offense was in operation in their lives.

I wish I had known that even when I tried to avoid conflict by being kind and respectful to others, there would still be those who would take me and my words out of context and twist the situation to their advantage. I was taught to treat people like I want to be treated, and I have always worked hard to live by those precepts. But even then, people get offended.

It has always amazed me to hear today's prophets speak about the end times. They talk about the wars and the rumors of wars, earthquakes in diverse places, and many other things that are mentioned in the Bible (Matthew 24:6). Jesus warned about these things when his disciples asked him about what signs to look for to indicate that the end is near.

But He also told them that *offense* would be one of the signs of the end times and coming of the Lord (Matthew 24:10). Well, my friend, from what I can see, the spirit of offense has caused many to stumble and to hold onto grudges. People are offended about the tiniest situations, so it doesn't have to be a major offense. Yes, it is the little foxes that spoil the vines (Song of Solomon 2:15), so we must guard our hearts from offense.

Jesus never walked in offense, even in his hour of great need. When He really needed a friend, Judas betrayed him.

When He asked the disciples to pray with Him in the Garden of Gethsemane on three separate occasions, they fell asleep on Him every time. And even when Peter denied Jesus three times after promising that he would die for Him, Jesus loved Peter anyway.

Jesus tells us to love our enemies, to bless those who curse us, to do good to those who hate us, and to pray for those who spitefully use and persecute us (Matthew 5:44). We need to do that even if we don't receive the same treatment in return. When I treat you right, it is not predicated on you treating me right in return; it's just the right thing to do.

When Joseph was abused by his brothers and sold into slavery, he could have held their ill-treatment against them. Instead, he forgave them because he realized that God had a plan for his life (Genesis 45). Joseph serves as an example of how we should live our lives as believers. Though it's not always easy, I choose to forgive others even before they hurt me. I encourage you to choose to do the same.

> *A brother offended is harder to be won than a strong city: and their contentions are like the bars of a castle.*
> —Proverbs 18:19

In the Old Testament, strong cities had walls around them that served as protection against invaders. The entrances used by the people were well-guarded and screened. If you owed taxes, you couldn't enter the city until they were paid. If you were a potential threat to the city, you were kept out.

We build walls of our own when we have been hurt to safeguard our hearts and prevent being wounded again. We push others away because we think they may try to hurt us; we choose to communicate only with people we feel are loyal, loving, and trustworthy; and we guard the gates to screen out those we don't know. We do all of these things to protect ourselves, but in the end, we discover that we have built our own prison.

In Israel, the Sea of Galilee receives water and gives it out; it's a body of water full of life, nurturing fish and plants. When the water leaves the Sea of Galilee, it is carried by way of the Jordan River to the Dead Sea, but the Dead Sea only takes water in and does not give it out. The same waters that supported fish and plants are unable to do so in the Dead Sea because living waters become dead waters when the two mix together. Similarly, Christians who walk in offense become like the Dead Sea as they allow the waters of offense to contaminate their hearts.

> *Then said he unto the disciples, it is impossible*
> *but that offences will come: but woe unto*
> *him, through whom they come!*
> —Luke 17:1

Offense will come! Count on it! And when it does, we must quickly repent, or it will manifest itself in horrible ways such as resentment, hurt, jealousy, anger, bitterness, strife, hatred, and envy.

## NOW THAT I KNOW

1. Who in your circle is easily and frequently offended?

   _____

   a. How do you feel when you are around that person?

   _____

   _____

   _____

   b. Do they have an actual cause for being offended or has it become a way of life?

   _____

   _____

   _____

   c. How can you help this person overcome offense?

   _____

   _____

   _____

d. What is the best way to deal with their frequent habit of being offended?

_____

_____

2. What does the Bible say about being offended?

_____

_____

_____

3. What Scriptures can help you handle others who are offended? Your own sense of being offended?

_____

_____

_____

4. How can you use a person's offense to inspire those around you?

_____

_____

_____

# CHAPTER 8

# I WISH THEY'D TOLD ME

## *That People Can Be Vicious*

While recently speaking at a revival service, I was asked by the pastor to go and visit a sick friend in the hospital, so we stopped by and said a prayer for him. During our visit with the man, he mentioned that he didn't understand why he was going through all these things, but that he felt the need to write a book about everything he was going through.

I tried to encourage him to follow through and write the book, and in the midst of our conversation, I asked him a few questions about what he was writing. I asked him to give me a list of ten things he wished he had known before he started pastoring. His wife laughed and told me that she could give me twenty to thirty!

I laughed and told her that he could just give me the short list.

To my surprise, the first thing out of his mouth was how he didn't know how people could be so vicious, mean, hateful, vindictive, and unforgiving. He added more to his list, but he kept coming back to his first answer. All I could say was that I completely agree with him. As he continued to share his feelings on the matter, he mentioned how his two sons hated the church and wanted absolutely nothing to do with it. I was caught off guard as I listened to this man share his heart, and I was in awe that he carried such a heavy load.

This pastor also told me how his wife was carrying a heavy load as well, and how she was dealing with numerous emotional scars which were hurting their marriage relationship. Unfortunately, to cope with carrying her burden, she had withdrawn from others and built walls around her life to protect herself.

As my friend poured out his heart while lying in that hospital bed, I found myself thinking about the many wounded warriors in the ministry who have shared similar stories of pain and heartache with me. It's a long list, and none of us in leadership know how to avoid vicious people, so we need to constantly be in a prayerful frame of mind as we seek the Lord's help to deal with the situations when they occur. I am so thankful that my friend opened his heart to share the challenges he was facing in his ministry.

I had another pastor share with me about his run to serve on the general board of a national organization. Amazingly, a group of people was opposed to seeing this man serve on the board, and they paid others to spread vicious rumors about him to discredit him. As a result, he considered withdrawing his name due to the politics of it all. But after receiving some wise counsel, he continued his campaign because he knew his character. Even though he went on to win the race, some of the rumors are still floating around, and he is still weathering that storm.

You've probably heard how the church army is the only one in the world that kills its own wounded. That is why I warn every young leader that whether they are a church leader or a business leader, that people can and will be vicious at times. No matter what you do to avoid it, you simply can't.

Jesus had enemies, the prophets had enemies, and we are going to have enemies, too. The question we must ask is: How do we prepare ourselves for something we're unable to see coming? The simple answer is prayer. We need to pray that God will shield us. That doesn't mean we won't face storms of viciousness, but God is faithful to see us through them. I am a living witness that proves this to be true.

When faced with vicious people, we need to learn how to walk away and find peace in our spirits. Leaders need to be careful not to become the thing that they hate and dislike in others.

If someone turns on you, you turn to God. Don't get bitter, get better. And remember, just because you may be through with the situation doesn't mean the situation is through with you.

Here are a few tips on what to do. I hope you'll find these helpful:

1. Let God vindicate you. Don't do to them what they did to you.
2. Ignore rumors. You will never get to the bottom of them.
3. Let God settle the issue. Don't take your brother to court.

Many of us have walked into ministry blindsided while feeling our way—afraid to take the next step, wishing all along that *if only I had a road map for ministry, it would be so much easier.* I heard the Christian leaders' cries of, "There are so many things I wish I knew or wish they had told me." And that's when I realized this feeling of wishing they'd been better prepared came fast, hard, and often and in more ways than even I could count.

## NOW THAT YOU KNOW

1. Think of a time when someone started vicious rumors about you that were not true.

   _____

   _____

   _____

   a. How did you handle the situation?

   _____

   _____

   _____

   _____

   b. What could you have done differently to get a different outcome?

   _____

   _____

   _____

   _____

c. What did you learn from that experience?

2. In your opinion, why do you think Christian people choose to act with malice toward their brothers and sisters in Christ?

3. How does the Bible tell us to handle these situations?

4. What Scriptures can we cling to for peace during trying times when God's people are vicious and unfair toward us?

5. How can your experiences inspire and benefit those around you?

_____

_____

_____

_____

# CHAPTER 9

# I Wish They'd Told Me

## *That There Will Be Drama*

> *Some people create their own storms*
> *then get mad when it rains.*
> —Unknown

If new ministers freshly called by God to pastor had known the extent of drama that was ahead for them, they might have decided to pursue different vocations. Drama can be an unfortunate part of life in a church family. Even the oldest, most stable congregations have members that often fight like siblings, or exaggerate even the most mundane event to create drama.

A friend shared a story about drama in her church. Two elderly widows were dating the same man. Many people in the church knew it, but failed to tell either woman that their intended was also dating their friend on the other end of the pew. He married one of the women, and she announced it in church the next Sunday, unaware that her husband had also been dating her friend. Everyone turned to the unchosen widow. She was shocked, angry, and emotional. This woman stood up and lectured the church members, telling them, "You are supposed to be my brothers and sisters in Christ, yet you all let me be taken for a fool!" The drama continued the following Sunday when the recently married woman brought her husband to church. He stood up and explained why he married one and not the other. "I love them both, but I didn't marry (name withheld) because she never slows down even at 86, she would have worked me to death!"

As church leaders, we cannot totally eliminate drama, but we can combat it in real ways. Here are some ideas that work:

1. Ask God to help you handle the situation. (Hebrews 4:16)
2. *A soft answer turneth away wrath: but grievous words stir up anger* (Proverbs 15:1). The Bible tells us specifically to speak softly to avoid ugly confrontations. That is an effective way to minimize drama, especially emotionally-charged angry drama. It is hard to escalate drama when your target responds without anger and refuses to engage in angry diatribes. Don't try to have the last word, and do not engage in tit-for-tat arguments.
3. Take a deep breath and don't overreact. Because someone else is emotional does not mean you have to invest in or contribute to their behavior. Keep a safe emotional distance to maintain objectivity.
4. Be constructive in your response to drama.
5. Walk away if necessary before it gets out of hand.
6. Control your own inclination to act out of a sense of drama. The Bible says, *So flee youthful passions and pursue righteousness, faith, love, and peace, along with those who call on the Lord from a pure heart* (II Timothy 2:22).
7. If drama includes anger, let it go by bedtime. (Ephesians 4:26)

8. Recognize when drama is concealed in a prayer request that stemmed from gossip.
9. Most drama can be directly addressed using Scriptures that cover the issue.
10. Remember the healing effects of forgiveness and its importance in resolving the drama.

Your church family is very much like a real family, warts and all. Some family members are more prone to drama than others, and some seem to thrive on it, finding excitement in the interchange of emotion. Ego and gossip are often parts of the drama equation, and poor judgement is normally involved as well. As a pastor, you are the church family's spiritual leader and it will fall on your shoulders to mediate drama when it occurs. Issues will arise in the church body and in the lives of believers, it is unavoidable. Remain calm, listen more than you talk, stay neutral if you can, and recommend forgiveness quickly.

## NOW THAT I KNOW

1. Who do you know that is always involved in some kind of drama?

   _____

   a. How do you feel when you are around this person?

   _____

   _____

   _____

   b. How do you handle it when the drama is brought to you as a church leader, or you are pulled into the drama as part of the cast?

   _____

   _____

   _____

   c. What could you do differently to get a different outcome?

   _____

   _____

   _____

d. How can you help this person need less drama?

_____

_____

_____

2. What does the Bible say about drama?

_____

_____

_____

3. What Scriptures can you find to help you deal with people who thrive on drama?

_____

_____

_____

4. How can you use episodes of drama to inspire others not to engage in it?

_____

_____

_____

# CHAPTER 10

# I Wish They'd Told Me

## *The Challenges and Burdens of Building and Business*

In my interviews with leaders, there was a wide range of questions from A to Z. The pages of this book only scratch the surface. I can't begin to tell you the burdens and the worries that are linked to building. Whether it's building a building, building people's lives, building confidence, building hope, or building morale, all can be challenging. On the one hand, there is a worry about all the details coming together or lining up. Whether you concern yourself about bills being paid on time, plans being followed, or perhaps plans being changed, you're constantly giving attention to details. It can be exciting, but on the other hand, it's very challenging. Time restraints, possible delays, or so many other things can hinder progress, and if you're not careful, you can become consumed with the projects. They can become overwhelming. I spoke with several pastors who confessed that they wanted to walk away in the middle of the project or even at the end of the project. They wanted to give up because of frustration. Jesus says that you have to count the cost.

Many shared with me that they only focused on the finished product and not the process because the process can cause you to have a nervous breakdown. Never go into a building program thinking it will go by the book. Sorry, you are sadly mistaken, even when you plan your work then work your plan.

Many felt the battle while they were building. One pastor said to me the moment he put the shovel in the ground for dedication and opened the earth, he felt like he opened up the pits of hell. Every spiritual attack was launched against him and his church.

The book of Nehemiah best describes how the spirit of opposition will come against you, or shall we say opposing spirits while building. As soon as Nehemiah organized a team and began to rebuild walls, notice in chapter 4 how people began to mock him and undermined the work. Saballat, Tobiah, and Geshem all came against him with a critical spirit. They mocked him and they will mock you, too.

Nehemiah never lost focus. He stuck to the vision. He armed and warned the people. He had a sword in one hand and a hammer in the other hand. While they were building, they were also battling. Remember to select a building committee to help offset the workload.

Exodus 18 describes how Moses tried to handle everything alone without help until his father-in-law Jethro gave him wise counsel:

> *And Moses' father in law said unto him,*
> *The thing that thou doest is not good. Thou wilt*
> *surely wear away, both thou, and this people that*
> *is with thee: for this thing is too heavy for thee;*
> *thou art not able to perform it thyself alone.*
> —Exodus 18: 17-18

You can't bear this burden alone, it's way too heavy for you. You shall surely wear away, you and your congregation.

There will always be warfare. It is linked to building. In Matthew 16:18, Jesus said that,

> *...upon this rock I will build my church; and the gates of hell shall not prevail against it.*

It's the unseen things, those unseen forces that come against you. The devil hates a building program because you are advancing the Kingdom of God.

I remember when we were starting our building projects. It seemed all hell broke loose. We were excited, but at the same time, we were fighting the enemy, all at the same time. I want to encourage you to keep pressing on as Nehemiah did in Chapter 6. When approached by opposers, he didn't get distracted. He stayed focused on the assignment. He said, "I'm on the wall doing a great work, and I will not come down." Determine to see it finished! You will have challenges but keep on building. Keep a hammer in one hand and a sword in the other – build and battle.

## The Business of Leadership

The Word of God instructs us that in business, we are to be men. There is a right way and a wrong way to conduct business. Here are some guidelines that make things run more smoothly when followed:

- Every business meeting long or short should always start with a prayer and end with a prayer, whether it is a 5-person meeting or 500-person meeting.

- Most pastors shared with me that for the most part their business meetings ran smoothly. But on the other hand, some nightmares occurred that escalated to anger, rage, or loud outbursts. There was one incident in which there was actually a fist fight inside the building because the one person thought another was withholding information. Acts 6:3 tells us how to select those who participate in the business of the church:

  *Wherefore, brethren, look ye out among you seven men of honest report, full of the Holy Ghost and wisdom, whom we may appoint over this business.*

- Have the right people working around money. Make sure they are honest and trustworthy.
- Everything that happens in church is not for public knowledge. It is not wise to reveal everything.

## NOW THAT I KNOW

1. What is your vision for the next five years?

   _____

   _____

   _____

   a. Is it realistic?

   _____

   b. What do you need to have in place to make it reality?

   _____

   _____

   _____

   c. What people do you need around you supporting your efforts?

   _____

   _____

   _____

d. Do you have the labor, equipment, and materials to complete the vision? If not, what do you still need to accomplish the vision? How will you acquire what is missing?

_____

_____

_____

2. How do the people on your board decide what is public and what is private information? Do you discuss it? Vote on it?

_____

_____

_____

3. How do you handle disagreements and opposing opinions among the leadership team? Are the outcomes desirable? Does something need to be changed? If so, what is it and how do you change it?

_____

_____

_____

4. How do you get rid of the naysayers in your midst who consistently oppose what God has called you to do?

_____

_____

_____

# CHAPTER 11

# I Wish They'd Told Me

## *The Importance of Rest*

While interviewing several pastors about some of their regrets, many expressed to me about the importance of sleep – good sleep, uninterrupted rest. I recall one pastor saying to never make a major decision without thinking it through or when you are tired. Make sure your mind and thoughts are clear (the old saying: Let me sleep on it). God anoints your speaking and your sleeping. There's nothing like sweet sleep and blessed rest.

Jesus said *come apart* and rest before you *fall apart*.

> *And he said unto them come ye yourselves*
> *apart into a desert place, and rest a while:*
> *for there were many coming and going,*
> *and they had no leisure so much as to eat.*
> —Mark 6:31

As leaders, we have a desire to pursue the works of God, but in doing so, we sacrifice much of our own time so that we may help others as God has called us to do. There are many qualities and characteristics of a leader, but commitment is one that holds great power. Leadership requires commitment, but not just any kind of commitment. There must be commitment within the secular world as well as the commitment to God in the spiritual realm. Each day brings new challenges, new chances, and a necessary fight that only God can bring forth through you. If you stay committed to the things of God both spiritually and in the secular world and always continue walking with a clear mind keeping Him as your primary focus of contact, He will provide the way for your future.

As leaders, we carry much responsibility and at times, even if we don't admit it, we need our rest. God requires us to rest, especially knowing all that we have had to take on in such a short amount of time. From the time we wake up until we close our eyes, we work for the Lord. The more you work for the God, the more opportunities will come. Because you are a willing vessel and a serving leader, others will give you work to do which will require you to rest from one opportunity to the next. With new endeavors, you will have long days and sleepless nights. Therefore, rest is important, not just in the physical world but in the spiritual realm as well.

> *Elisha was running from Jezebel*
> *and he fell asleep under the juniper tree.*
> *Even after he ate he fell asleep again.*
> —1 Kings 19:4-8

Studies show that excessive sleepiness can hurt work performance, wreak havoc on relationships, and lead to mood problems like anger and depression. Most people don't understand the effect that too little rest can have on their cognitive and mental health. Quite frankly, this is a serious matter regarding leadership, especially when more than one leader is struggling with it at the same time. Leaders should not be worrying about inability to focus. If you are not able to concentrate on what is at hand due to lack of rest, how are you going to lead others in a manner that is suitable in the circumstances?

Did you know that the lack of rest and sleep can hinder you from thinking clearly and keeping your emotions in tune with God? It is vital as a leader to value the importance of your rest outside of leadership. A leader is not someone who acts as a leader for only a brief period, but a leader is someone who maintains his position throughout the day and night. How can we be effective leaders in this generation if we cannot love ourselves enough to know when to take time for ourselves?

Sleepiness slows down your thought process. Scientists have found that sleep deprivation leads to lower alertness and concentration which means that it is more difficult for leaders to focus on the task at hand, especially when it involves others. This gives the enemy easy access, and we all know that we must keep ourselves protected at all times, for our lives and well-being depends on it.

As leaders, God wants us to have logical reasoning, and at times we must be capable of thinking outside the box. Without the appropriate amount of rest, how can God use us effectively? How are we supposed to reach others and allow God to use us to help lead the way when we can't even tell one foot from another? We learned to follow, therefore, we are able lead, but what about the leaders above us? Without enough rest, can we be trusted by our leaders to make the right decisions? You cannot assess situations appropriately if not well rested. You might get the job done, but how much better could you have done? When you are too tired, you often don't do what God wanted you to do. Instead you settle for your own way (which may be mediocre) because you are just too tired for excellence.

Memory is an important factor in the Body of Christ, especially in leadership. We must remember the guidelines that have been set forth before us, Scriptures that need to be discussed, and rules and regulations that promote order. To be great leaders, we must learn to work in order. Memory becomes an effective tool regarding order and presenting order as it should be. Not having enough rest and sleep can impair your memory, which we do not want in our leaders. We cannot allow any damage to occur within our mental state because we are not taking care of ourselves. Research suggests that the nerve connections that make our memories are strengthened during sleep. Resting gives us more of a chance at learning and remembering what we are asked to do.

Have you ever been given a job to do and someone spoke to you thinking that you were listening? Then they walked away, only for you to be left there wondering what it is that you really are supposed to be doing? That happens when you are not rested. When tired, you were not ready to listen and allow your memory to work.

You are less likely to pick up new information without rest. You are also less likely to feel the Holy Spirit moving in you and even in the atmosphere in which His presence is known. Why do you think that at times others can feel God's presence, but you cannot? Focus-driven leaders learn to make time for themselves, knowing that rest is an important factor of growth and their journey with God. One of the responsibilities of a leader is to retain information and use that as fuel to energize someone else. Brothers and sisters, we cannot have slow reaction times. Without the appropriate amount of rest, we react slower than what is expected of us. You wouldn't want to be asked to pray for someone but not know what to say because of fatigue. As a leader, you are held accountable for everyone that you pray for or fellowship with. The last thing you want to do as a leader is to cause someone to stumble or hold them back because of your ignorance. How are you supposed to help others and be a support system when you can't even pick yourself up to do your work or the tasks that are required of you? Quick response leaders!

Your mood as a leader can make you or it can break you. Lack of sleep can alter your mood significantly causing irritability and anger, and may even lessen your ability to cope with stress. Lord knows as leaders, we have enough stress to last us years down the road, but we choose not to live in our stress. We would not be able to handle the requirements of leadership if we were depressed and oppressed all the time. Sleepiness puts you at greater risk for depression because they are so closely connected. Sleep specialists aren't always sure which comes first in their patients due to the closeness of the two.

Now, sleep and your mood can affect one another. The best way to know whether you are getting enough rest is by how you feel. You should not feel sleepy when you wake in the morning, and you should be energized throughout the day and then slowly wind down as you approach your bedtime. An important question to ask yourself is, "Is my performance where I want it to be?" Your performance and your rest are crucial to your day-to-day activities and quality of life. Don't rush through your life. We tend to rush through life allowing our days to connect with our nights with no possibility of rest in between. God wants us to make time to hear Him, and we often run out of time and energy for that. If we are just doing our job all the time and listening to just those in the secular world, how are we to make time to listen to the Father?

To lead others, we must first take care of ourselves. How can we lead others to higher levels both physically and spiritually without first showing them the effective way to do so? Success comes in many shapes and sizes, but rest plays an important role in the lives of a leader. Every day is a challenge for a leader, and with every challenge, you must sacrifice your time and your energy. In doing so, you must learn when to renew yourself and replenish what has been used or lost. God sacrificed His time for six days creating the beautiful world in which we live, but on the seventh day, He chose to rest. God knew that even though He had much work to do, that rest was needed at the time of completion. There are so many things competing for your attention, which is why it is so important for leaders to have self-control. This involves knowing when to rest and when to work.

One of the most crucial elements of a good leader is maintaining a balanced life. For without it, how can we find the strength to keep moving forward and remain in it? How many sleepless nights have you had, then noticed the next day that you were walking in your own emotions? It is hard to walk in the Spirit and be driven by God in truth when you can't even hold yourself together. As a leader, you must value your rest because without it, you will not be able to manage your time well. Time management is important in the Body of Christ, specifically when we talk about leadership. God knows that you can't do it all by yourself. People who rest on a regular basis have better results than those who don't. As leaders, we are busy, and there is a lot to get done. But if God can make time to rest and prioritize His efforts, so can you!

Spending time away from work-related things is also something that helps you rest as leaders. It is just like studying for an exam. After a certain amount of time, the instructor will insist that you get your head out of the book for a little bit, and go do something else. This equips you to be able to think better later, and helps get your brain back on the level that it should be. Leadership works the same way: You need to take time for just yourself and rest outside of your duties and responsibilities. Without proper rest and relaxation, how are you going to slow down enough to know what God wants you to do next? Leaders are supposed to allow God to lead them, but He can't if they are always moving and never giving Him the chance to renew and revise their mind as well as illuminate them mentally, physically, and spiritually.

As a leader, you understand that the things still to be done can take a toll on your heart, but you must understand that God will give you peace during the battle if you let him. The battles of everyday life as a leader can be tough, and it can be hard to find the positive among all the chaos. However, with rest, God will give you the strength to handle it. Most of us want some form of satisfaction of having things taken care of, but sometimes, we must learn to trust in others and learn how to delegate some of the responsibilities so that we can get the rest needed to come back and finish the work that God has set before us.

We need time to rebuild and recover from overwork and burnout. God asks us to make time to regroup ourselves. God requires from us our very best, so without rest, we cannot give God our very best. When leaders feel as though everything depends on them, or they think everything starts and finishes with them, they become exhausted and overwhelmed at times. Don't let that be you! Learn to let go and give God the opportunity to work on your behalf to restore you for the future. God will never give you more than you can bear, but He does ask you to give yourself rest to be able to continue in the things of Him, which require work, time, and energy.

In my research, I came across this and I found it to be true, "We remain confined within the limits of our minds unless we turn to the divine reality for pardon." When we learn who we are, we achieve true mental clarity in the spiritual realm. Taking rest gives us the ability to learn who we really are, which helps us on our own journey with God. When we are not doing for others, we need to find quiet time just to do for ourselves. How can we find out who we are and claim our mental clarity if our minds, bodies, and souls are not functioning properly and in order due to lack of rest?

Spirituality is integrated into our everyday life, not just in worship and prayer. Many do not realize that our spiritual lives (or lack of) may be causing some of our health issues including our inability to rest. Our bodies, minds, emotions, and energy levels form us into the people we are. It is only by dealing with each part of ourselves that we can be used fully and effectively. Our thoughts and emotions cause reactions in the body. When people think of comfort and having fun or when they are feeling hopeful, chemicals are released through the parasympathetic nervous system causing relaxation and promoting healing. When feeling angry, adrenaline and other neurotransmitters are released through the sympathetic nervous system causing stress and agitation. If we as leaders do not get enough rest physically and spiritually, we will not be at God's best and can fail in works and prayer to do what God has called us to do.

One of the spiritual disciplines we must practice is discovering what particular things, experiences, or relationships can help us overcome the barriers we face due to lack of rest. As a Christian, we are to love one another as

God loves us, and leaders must continuously walk in love. You will have a hard time thinking, feeling, and acting like Jesus when you lack the desire to take care of your needs and rest. "An article in New York Time says, 'America has a sleep deficit that is worse than the national deficit, and it results in everything from increased irritability to fatal car accidents.'" (A Gift from God, 2017). Sleep is a gift from God!

> *I will both lie down and sleep in peace;*
> *for you alone, O Lord, make me lie down in safety.*
> —Psalm 4:8

Taking time to rest is an act of trust in God. The world remains in God's hands, and when we put our faith into motion, it makes it easy to take out time for ourselves to rest trusting that God will wake us up in the morning and continue finishing what we have started. "Elijah was to spend a prolonged time in solitude and prayer at Mount Horeb. The angel of the Lord had him take not one, but two naps. Contrast this with the disciples at Gethsemane, who could not pray because they kept falling asleep." (Ortberg, 2002). Leaders, value your rest, and God will value your time.

> *It is vain for you to rise up early, to sit up late,*
> *to eat the bread of sorrows: for so*
> *he giveth his beloved sleep.*
> —Psalm 127:2

## NOW THAT I KNOW

1. What signs would you look for to indicate that you are deprived of adequate sleep?

   _____

   _____

   _____

2. Think of five ways you can add more rest and relaxation to your life.

   a. _____

   b. _____

   c. _____

   d. _____

   e. _____

3. What are five ways you can add more sleep to your schedule?

   a. _____

   b. _____

   c. _____

d. _____

e. _____

4. What changes in your personality and motivation take place when you do not get enough sleep for a long period of time?

   _____

   _____

   _____

5. Why do you think God places such a premium on sleep?

   _____

   _____

   _____

# EPILOGUE

# I Wish They Told Me

## *And the List Goes On . . .*

Although many statements were made and some personal experience shared—some I can mention and some I can't so as to protect the innocent—they are by no means the only way the enemy tries to steal our good names and the good we are doing through our ministries. Remember, the sly old devil has more tricks up his sleeve than he can show us in our lifetimes. Here's just a sampling of what to be on the lookout for.

- If you run, sooner or later you'll get tired. You may trip up, but just get back up and get in the race.
- If you own or run a business, people are going to steal from you: both customers and employees.
- If you are a horse trainer, sooner or later you're going to be bucked off the horse or even get kicked by a horse.
- If you're a boxer, not only will you learn how to throw a punch but you better learn how to take a hit. It comes with the territory.
- If you are a dentist, you will eventually get a toothache. Doctors get sick, too.
- If you are a speaker, preacher, and teacher, there are times you will get butterflies. I remember going

to my pastor and asking him to pray for me that I would not be nervous anymore when I preached. At the time twenty-five years ago, I had been preaching for at least seven years, so I thought the nervousness and butterflies should have been over by then. But I remember the wisdom my pastor imparted to me that day. His response was, "No, son, I'm not praying that prayer. You need to feel that so you won't depend on your own knowledge or strength or intellect. But your dependency will be totally on God." Now that was great wisdom for me.

- If you are a parent, your kids will at some time break your heart into a thousand pieces.
- If you are married, you'll become discouraged now and then, and disagreements will happen, but through respectful dialogue, you can work through anything. Remember that it is okay for you or your spouse to get mad, just try not to get mad at the same time. Give your spouse room to be human and less than perfect.
- If you are a quarterback in football, sooner or later you're going to get sacked. If you stand on truth, you won't be accepted by many, but at least you know about it. And so it is in ministry; you will be misunderstood, lied to, mislabeled, abused, persecuted, neglected, and rejected. I wish they had told me that you can do everything right and still be crucified on a cross.
- I wish they told me not to chase down rumors because you don't have to prove anything to your friends, and your enemies won't believe you anyhow.
- A pastor is not just there to simply preach. A pastor's job involves so much more than that. You'll have to deal with all kinds of "stuff" before you head to the

pulpit. Then, there will be more stuff to deal with from the office.
- Not everyone's advice is good advice. Yes, there is safety in a multitude of counselors (Proverbs 11:14), but make sure that you are listening to wise counsel.
- Sometimes the great sacrifices you and your family have to make will rob you of family time. Helping others can sometimes hurt you.
- Ministry is a marathon, not a sprint. Galatians 5:7 says, *"Ye did run well; who did hinder you that ye should not obey the truth?"*
- You don't vote on vision; you follow vision.
- Your success will breed jealousy and hatred, as well as create enemies.
- Tradition can kill or destroy a church, keep it in stagnation, and freeze success.
- Expect to encounter loneliness, isolation, and feelings of rejection. Look to these examples as your inspiration to get you through: Jesus in the Garden, Jesus in the Wilderness, and Jesus on the Cross.
- Betrayal can be the most painful part of ministry. I call these situations "heart rippers." Jesus experienced it with Judas. Paul experienced it with Denias. David and Job experienced it with their friends.
- Those who start with you won't always stay with you. They left Jesus after hearing Jesus say to his own disciples that they would leave him.
- Expect spiritual warfare. Jesus said, *"These things I have spoken unto you, that in me ye might have peace. In the world ye shall have tribulation: but be of good cheer; I have overcome the world."* In this world, you're going to have tribulations, personal attacks against your marriage,

against your ministry, and against your health, but be of good cheer and overcome.
- Show me a Moses—I'll show you a Pharaoh.
- Show me an Elijah—I'll show you Ahab and Jezebel.
- Show me David—I'll show you a Saul.
- Outlive a lie and false accusations. Joseph went to prison on an accusation, not an action.
- Forgive people who have hurt you before you get bitter.
- The power of temptations—Money, sex, and power are influential enemies. Jesus was tempted (Luke 4). Samson and Solomon were also tempted, as was virtually every hero in the Bible.
- You've got to have compassion for the hurting man on Jericho road, who was left dying in his blood. Both a priest and a Levite saw him and walked on. A good Samaritan stopped to help this man. We see a dying and hurting society today, but do we do anything about it? When Jesus saw the multitude, he was moved with compassion. Are we moved with compassion?
- Your waiting is never a waste. You've got to be patient. Tarry wait; verbalize it, visualize it, and crystalize it.
- Your preparation through never-ending study will show yourself approved for the job. Training for reigning. Learning now but leading later.
- Competition will always bring on opposition.
- Don't lose focus or become distracted (Nehemiah 6). Teach yourself to be focus-driven.

I finally leave you with this statement: His mercy outweighs our mistakes. Remember that the only way to fight all opposition like a true Christian man is *on bended knee*.

# REFERENCES

A Gift from God. (n.d.). Retrieved June 19, 2017, from http://www.christianitytoday.com/moi/2002/003/june/gift-from-god.html

Edwards, J. (2013). *Charity and its fruits*. Pensacola, FL: Chapel Library.

Mack, G. (1959). I've been everywhere. [Recorded by Hank Snow, 1962]. On *The Essential Hank Snow* [Album]. New York: RCA Records.

Mcgettigan, C., Walsh, E., Jessop, R., Agnew, Z. K., Sauter, D. A., Warren, J. E., & Scott, S. K.

(2013). Individual Differences in Laughter Perception Reveal Roles for Mentalizing and

Sensorimotor Systems in the Evaluation of Emotional Authenticity. *Cerebral*

*Cortex, 25*(1), 246-257. doi:10.1093/cercor/bht227

Ortberg, J. (2002). The Life You've Always Wanted: Spiritual Disciplines for Ordinary People.

# ABOUT THE AUTHOR

Appearing on the Jim Bakker Show, Daystar, CBN, TBN, TCT, The God Channel, and DirecTV, Dr. Ron Webb is a prolific writer, speaker, teacher, and the pastor of the Mt. Calvary Powerhouse Church in Poplar Bluff, Missouri. Pastor Webb has been in the ministry for over 30 years. He attended Three Rivers College in Poplar Bluff where he majored in Business Administration and was a former "Raider" basketball player. He earned his Bachelor of Theology degree from the International College of Bible Theology, and a Master Degree of Pastor Studies in Counseling, and a Doctorate of Theology from Midwest Theological Seminary. Dr. Webb also had the honor of doing the invocation at the inauguration of Missouri Governor Jay Nixon. The unique ministry of Dr. Ron Webb is evident as he is anointed in the areas of church leadership and governance.

Dr. Webb has been considered by many to be "A Pastor to Pastors." His ministry is centered on restoration and racial reconciliation and a sincere belief that we must teach the lost at any cost. His preaching and teaching focus on empowerment and hope.

Dr. Webb is CEO and President of *S.E.M.O. Christian Restoration Center*, a place for individuals who need a second chance in life. He is founder and lead instructor of *School of the Prophets Bible College* in Poplar Bluff, Missouri. Students leave this Bible college as trained and experienced leaders ready to fulfill Jesus' command in Matthew 28:19 to "go ye therefore, and teach all nations."

# LOOK FOR THESE OTHER TITLES BY BISHOP RON WEBB

In *Leadership From Behind the Scenes*, Dr. Ron Webb provides Biblically-based advice to assist ministers from all faiths in their role as leaders in God's kingdom. Ministers are called to lead, to counsel and to encourage, but sometimes need the same guidance in their lives. This book will help ministers understand the challenges of church leadership, and how to become better shepherds and Christians as they live a life of service to others.

***Leadership From Behind the Scenes Group Study Workbook*** is intended to be a companion to Dr. Ron Webb's wonderful book, ***Leadership From Behind the Scenes***, this workbook has been designed as a teaching tool in a classroom setting. This guide book, when used while reading and studying ***Leadership From Behind the Scenes***, will help the reader extract critical points, take away real-world lessons and plans of action, and encourage lively discussions and discourse about some of the timely and sometimes sensitive points Dr. Webb makes us address.

Racism is not a skin problem, it is a **SIN** problem. Bishop Webb preaches that violence begets violence, but unity with the brethren will always invite the Holy Spirit in. Recognizing that you can be angry and sin not, Dr. Webb believes that righteous anger turns ordinary people into heroes who shape the course of history. He invites us to be part of the solution, and urges those hurt by racism not to let the adversity destroy their character, but instead let it define their character. Consistency is powerful, and Dr. Webb opens our eyes to the consistent opportunities to stand firm in our conviction that if God is no respecter of person, we should follow His example and embrace our differences with Christ-like love.

Spirits are real, both good and evil. God is a spirit, and the Devil operates from the spirit world. Ephesians 6:12 tells us, "For we wrestle not against flesh and blood, but against principalities, against powers, against the rulers of the darkness of this world, against spiritual wickedness in high places." Paul says not to be ignorant of Satan's many devices.

These powers operate inside the church. The more on fire a person is for God, the more spiritual warfare they are likely to encounter. We are the watchmen for the Kingdom. It's our responsibility, as well as our privilege, to sound the alarm and protect our Christian brothers and sisters.

This book exposes many of the evil spirits used by the enemy to derail, sidetrack, and afflict God's family.

www.ingramcontent.com/pod-product-compliance
Lightning Source LLC
Chambersburg PA
CBHW070240090526
44586CB00035B/1359